CHAMBORD

Five Centuries of Mystery

CHAMBORD

Five Centuries of Mystery

Text and photography
JEAN-MICHEL TURPIN

Foreword
STÉPHANE BERN

Introduction
JEAN D'HAUSSONVILLE

ABRAMS/NEW YORK

"Take a closer look,
and what you will see
is no longer what you have just seen."

Leonardo da Vinci

STÉPHANE BERN

The throngs of visitors who pass through the doors and gates of iconic French historic sites every September during the *Journées du patrimoine* (Heritage Days) confirm our national passion for cultural legacies. At a crossroads, each one of us is seeking orientation toward an uncertain future by drawing upon our past, our roots and our identity, engraved in ancient stones subsisting as traces of our collective memory.

It is about time that we become more aware of the symbolic import of our heritage, which also represents a major asset in the construction of tomorrow's France. The built historical heritage of our country must neither be fossilized nor frozen in time; on the contrary, it is called upon to evolve, to move with the times, to adapt as much as it can to the demands of our epoch, to unrestrictedly enter the twenty-first century, to wholeheartedly embrace the new norms of accessibility and exigencies of sustainability . . . without surrendering its soul. Our monuments are not solely a perpetually open invitation to reverie and wonder at the beauty brought into being by human hands, but also serve as invaluable testimony to the past and as an inexhaustible source of benefits for the future. In a country that remains the most visited in the world, with ninety million tourists a year, our heritage represents an unhoped-for opportunity, a veritable gold mine, a dream factory, as well as an economic boon, and one of the many advantages of this treasure for tourism is that it cannot be outsourced or delocalized!

When our tongues quiet down because we have ceased to learn, telltale stones continue to speak. They recount who we are and where we come from; they attest to formidable human adventures insofar as they were fulcrums of technological revolutions, unveiling daring creativity and singular innovatory talents.

As we draw near the five hundredth anniversary of the Renaissance, the château of Chambord remains its most fascinating and intriguing example. In its very essence, intrinsically forward-looking, it expresses perpetual renewal; at the same time, its exceptional integrity renders it strikingly close to its original state, and its architectural conception bespeaks an intelligence and perfection in which the inspiration and genius of Leonardo da Vinci are there to be detected.

In its construction, ordered by François I on September 6, 1519, Chambord sends us a message of hope, the perspective of an eternal renaissance.

If I expressed the wish to sponsor this magnificent book on the occasion of the five hundredth anniversary of Chambord, I did so in a frame of mind focused on the present, in the context of the national heritage inventory mission with which the president of the Republic has entrusted me. I was determined to render homage to the work Chambord has striven to accomplish to prepare for this half-millennium, maintaining the status of our country while economizing on public funds. To put it another way, Chambord has accommodated the necessities of modern life without in any way bartering away its soul or muting its poetry.

Yes, today's Chambord provides proof that mobilization for our heritage can succeed and that rather than representing a burden or a budgetary expense, our monuments are above all an investment for the future, and a rare opportunity for France.

CHAMBORD,
SPIRIT AND GENIUS

A work of genius, conveyor of a universal language, Chambord is a unique monument that remains in many respects unknown.

Chambord defies the imagination by superimposing several key meanings: a political edifice, a spiritual and metaphysical construction, a hunters' lodge and a renowned castle. Placed as early as 1850 on the initial list of French historic monuments, on an equal footing with the Louvre or Versailles, and later catalogued by UNESCO as a World Heritage site, Chambord, with its false symmetry and many unknowns, is the most mysterious royal palace of them all.

How are we to reinterpret an enigmatic monument while ensuring the conservation of an imposing estate? These two priorities have come together on the eve of the five hundredth anniversary of the beginnings of Chambord.

In 2019, we will celebrate the half-millennium of the start of construction, in 1519, of one of the most emblematic monuments of our country.

Five hundred years later, Chambord continues to occasion admiration and fascination. It is high time to deliver the keys that will allow Chambord to be deciphered as it was dreamed up and thought out by François I and Leonardo da Vinci. It behooves us to recreate the initial vision and render visible the original matrix of Chambord—that is to say a matrix at once material (the building) and immaterial (its symbols). Contrary to the received idea of a hunting lodge, Chambord was designed as an ideal city. The monument and the estate in its entirety are equally constitutive of its unity. At heart, the project in which we are engaged adheres to the idea of utopia at work.

Chambord is a monument of beauty and intelligence. Chambord is the quintessence of the Renaissance, not only because it is the most important civil building of its epoch, but also because its design and symbolism express the idea of perpetual renewal, of the life cycle, of mankind's place in the cosmos and of a form of eternity.

Even though the blueprint for Chambord was elaborated step by step with sizable input from several persons surrounding François I, the French monarch was the one and only founding patron, and few other royal castles display comparable unity of conception and realization. An ardent desire for unity is reflected in the overall layout of the estate, encircled and enclosed by walls that were planned from the outset by François I and completed in their existing form in 1650 by Gaston, duke of Orléans, brother of Louis XIII.

Given the rare prescience of an enigmatic genius and the awareness of a work completed according to its overall design, it is perhaps no surprise that all of France's political regimes have respected the architectural composition of the monument and the organic unicity of the estate. When Louis XIV applied the finishing touches, he was fulfilling the plan of François I, and over the ensuing centuries, no additional construction has occurred. In a way, Chambord is the anti-Fontainebleau insofar as it is neither a royal residence nor a labyrinthine palace, but rather a radically singular work of art, the only one of its kind. As a major European movement, as an early manifestation of globalization, and as the initial revolution of the cultural industries, the Renaissance represents the first stage of a process leading to contemporary societies; it portends individuation and freedom to think, to believe, to desire and to opine—that is to say the values enshrined in the Universal Declaration of Human Rights.

If Chambord is essential to the heritage of mankind, this is due not only to its incomparable, genially inspired beauty, but also to its having been derived from a universalist conception of humanity that speaks to each and every one of us. That is why Chambord, one of the first French historic monuments, has held its place since 1981 on the UNESCO list, prior to being joined by the Loire, a river revered by more than one poet.

In 1930, having acquired the estate in its entirety, the French Republic made an irreversible choice, and for the past eighty-eight years the integrity of the vast property—the château, the village, the forest and the twenty miles of surrounding walls—has been painstakingly maintained. And step by step, the State has come to favor unified management enabling establishment of a national public body, placed under the high protection of the president of the Republic by dint of a February 2005 law pertaining to the development of rural territories in France.

Today this public body is invested with the mission of enabling a broadened public to discover or rediscover an enigmatic and little-known Chambord, whose conceptual power bridges five centuries, while its poetry continues to enchant the young.

That is the alpha and omega of today's efforts: to better accommodate a public having come from throughout France and all over the world—and to do so in accordance with the principles of sustained development and in view of providing enhanced access to one of the most accomplished works of humanity. As the National Estate of Chambord welcomes more and more visitors and becomes increasingly self-financing, projects of prime importance are being launched so as to set before the visitor's eyes a radically transformed and magnified Chambord.

> **"If Chambord is essential to the heritage of mankind, this is due not only to its incomparable, genially inspired beauty, but also to its having been derived from a universalist conception of humanity that speaks to each and every one of us"**

The objective is not to organize ephemeral festivities during a year of rejoicing, but rather to carry out a perennial investment aimed at renewing interpretation of Chambord.

Among the many ongoing projects, three stand out, and they form a triptych: *The Chambord, 1519–2019, Utopia at Work* exhibition is being organized by two commissioners: while the philosopher Roland Schaer will delve into the genesis of Chambord and demonstrate its "Vincian" origins, the architect Dominique Perrault will ask twenty schools of architecture scattered over five continents to answer a fictitious question on the contemporary architectural completion of Chambord by means of digital mockups.

Restoration of the cupola-shaped lanterns and their gold plating: the objective is to burnish the summit of the lanterns and bring back into view the lead ornaments as they were in 1539 upon the arrival of Charles V. Taken together, they will constitute the external, spectacular and poetic signal of the heavenly nature of the ideal city. They will recall the books of chivalry that inspired François I and the element of surprise he desired, which still works its charm as the visitor discovers, deep in the woods, as in a fairy tale, an astonishing monument.

Installation in the château of an itinerant court reminiscent of the one that accompanied François I during his many journeys: the visitor will be welcomed as though he were the king's guest, and by entering a recreated itinerant court, he will be initiated to its lifestyle up until the times of Louis XIV in Versailles. This is the first reconstitution of its kind; there exists no equivalent elsewhere in France. We are also attending to the interior rearrangement and refurbishing of Chambord in view of achieving enhanced coherency and rendering a visit even more exciting and enticing.

Chambord is the grandest Renaissance château in the world. Its architectural power is such that not one of the sovereigns succeeding François I ever altered its envelope of stone. Contrary to numerous royal castles, no new wing or section has been added to or made to replace an original component. To this very day, its mysterious aura remains intact. By ascending the double helix staircase, following in the footsteps of François I, Catherine de' Medici, Louis XIV, Molière and, more recently, Victor Hugo, we take a journey at once into and out of time. And when we reach the overlying terraces, the view of a heavenly village is altogether breathtaking. With this book, we are proposing an unprecedented voyage in the history of Chambord from the highly informed perspective of Jean-Michel Turpin, who spent two years with us. On the lookout for moments to capture, he offers a vision of Chambord that is at once intimate, realistic . . . and more than a little surprising. As we look forward to the upcoming five hundred years . . .

Jean d'Haussonville
General director of the National Estate of Chambord

CONTENTS

A DREAM OF STONE IN UNTAMED NATURE

"Having ordered the construction of a handsome and majestic edifice in lieu and place of Chambord . . . "

Ordinance of François I, September 1519

Cambo-ritos: in Celtic, "crossing of the ford." Indeed, it was with a small ford in a bend of the Cosson, a minor tributary meandering alongside the Loire, a little less than ten miles east of Blois, that the name "Chambord" originated. To the north, between the minor and the major rivers, there were marshy and frequently flooded prairies; to the south, there was the game-rich forest of Sologne. While Chambord had come into existence well before the Gallic period, life in those precincts was harsh and the air humid and unhealthy, a breeding ground for diseases. The first evidence of a dwelling dates back to the late twelfth century, when the counts of Blois had a number of hunting lodges built in the vicinity: Montrion in the forest of Russy, Bury in the forest of Blois, the more ancient Montfrault in the forest of Boulogne and, finally, Chambord. Nestled amidst reeds and oak trees, encased by a church and a village, a small medieval castle with at least two towers and a drawbridge appeared.

In 1515, when he succeeded Louis XII, François I was but twenty years old. Just six months after his coronation, he concluded the Battle of Marignano triumphantly. At the peak of his glory, he strove to embody power and prowess in opposition to the Europe of Charles V, Holy Roman Emperor, and Henry VIII of England. He became known as the King Chevalier. Back from Italy, he took to sojourning in Chambord with his entourage, not far from the royal residences in Amboise and in Blois where he had dwelt as a child. It was in Chambord that he could frolic around his favorite hunting grounds, which were teeming with game and spacious enough for him to feel far from the outside world. Fully immersed in nature, he would hunt down the "red and black beasts," the stags and the boars, while herons and salamanders lingered nearby.

In late 1516, Leonardo da Vinci arrived in France at the invitation of the young monarch, who tasked him with transforming Romorantin, the capital of Sologne, into the capital of the kingdom. In 1519, the year of the Italian master's death, an epidemic struck the town and put an end to the project. Notwithstanding these two events, the king retained a pervasive desire to amaze, to astonish, to create something truly exceptional: a dream of stone in the unspoiled nature he so unstintingly adored. He was left with the houses sketched for pleasure offered by Leonardo, whose notebooks were likewise highly instructive. The architect king chose the shores of the Cosson, with its outdated fortress and depopulated village, as his building site. On September 6, 1519, he ordered the construction of "a handsome and majestic edifice in lieu and place of Chambord."

At first he named François de Pontbriand as project superintendent, but Pontbriand immediately desisted and delegated the assignment to Mathurin Viart, master accountant and controller of the Blois project, who was to be assisted by Jacques Sourdeau, master mason. The following month, the king was already busy supervising the construction kickoff. He took it upon himself to delimit the perimeters of the park and to stake out the borders of the future estate, a forest covering more than six thousand acres. In 1523, wishing to preserve nearby game and keep intruders out, he began to build a wall of stone in the northern section. The old and aging edifice was torn down. Foundations for the new edifice were laid down on water-logged and unstable soil. This phase of the labor proceeded through 1524. Twenty-six years later, Ambassador Giovanni Soranzo wrote:

"The foundations have been fashioned like houses in Venetia, propped up by stakes, with stones to be added later." The long-held idea that Chambord had been built on stilts was given renewed credence in 1984 on the occasion of in-depth probes allowing the architect Pierre Lebouteux to conclude: "The sub-structure of the foundations consists of slabs and stilts at a depth of 5.20 meters (17 feet), permanently immersed on a pure limestone bed." However, subsequent to the 2006 and 2007 excavations in the castle courtyard, a more accurate interpretation is now possible; the foundations may represent applications of a technique similar to the one utilized during antiquity and described in Vitruvius's *On Architecture*, a reference work for sixteenth-century builders. He suggested use of cement with pozzolan, a sand of volcanic origin. And when there was no sand available, he proposed a divider consisting of "two rows of stakes, firmly attached with strong bands to the chosen space, and the interval [between the stakes] will be filled with white loam transported in marsh grass sacks." Given the properties of the clay, the divider would form a hermetic barrier permitting "to empty out the remaining water between the two dikes, and once that space had been dried, to dig foundations down to solid ground, where the large hard filler stones known as *libages* would be jointed together with clay and sand." In soft soil, Vitruvius recommended "stilts of half-burned alder wood or olive or oak wood, the gaps between which would be filled with coal." Recent research has demonstrated that a similar technique was applied in Chambord. At a depth of 5.50 meters (18 feet), fragments of stakes sunk into the surrounding sediment and narrowly sectioned wood have been found, indicating the existence of vertical wattle partially contained in the foundation masonry. At the bottom, the foundations sealed off an invert of three by eight-centimeter (one by three-inch) bundles of wood placed on the substrate; they did not necessarily have a structural function, but may simply have prevented workers from wading through the mud. Moreover, the water may not have been deep enough to allow application of instructions as highly elaborated as Vitruvius's. In any event, the small dikes were filled successively with a mass of large stones and Beauce limestone blocks mixed with a mortar bed (thickness: 1.20 meters [4 feet]). This base was leveled off with a fifteen-centimeter (six-inch) mortar layer. An initial substructure of large blocks rose to a height of 1.70 meters (5 feet, 7 inches) and a final level of substructure consisting of small-sized limestone rubble rising to 1.80 meters (5 feet, 11 inches) and having little or nothing to do with the legendary stilts completed these solid foundations, thanks to which the building would emerge not so much from the soil, as from waters.

When creating the estate, François I determined its boundaries and had a wall built. Today, the twenty-mile wall still surrounds an estate of a size equivalent to Paris.

LANDS ABOUNDING
IN GAME

——

The estate's soil is mainly sandy or loamy. Carving out its bed, the Cosson has enabled the emergence of Beauce limestone underground and west of the forest, while parts of the low-lying alluvions of the Loire have covered the northwestern portion with sand and loam. The flat topography and the loamy soil have proved conducive to the formation of swamps, pools and ponds, of which a dozen appear on the estate. During the reign of François I, only the southern section of the park was wooded, whereas the north was essentially occupied by farmland; as late as the nineteenth century, there were twenty-three farms, just two of which remain today. An abundance of game in the Chambord area was surely a determinant factor in the king's choice. A varied landscape containing oak trees and plantations of pines, heaths, prairies and wetlands renders the forest unusually rich and ensures optimal living conditions for numerous animal species. Even today the stag, emblematic figure of the estate, continues to thrive.

Facing page: In the heart of the largest European enclosed forest, animals reside in the wild, in protected territory.

Following double-page: In the dried-up Neuf pond, herons come to fish.

Above: A large stag enters the Comte Thibault prairie.

Right-hand page: The pond known as l'étang Neuf.

Above: A stag drinks from
the pond known as La Baquetière.

Facing page: At La Canardière,
the Cosson flows into the canal.

"The place is located in the midst of
this marshland, surrounded by dead water."

Giovanni Soranzo, 1550

A PORT
ON THE
LOIRE

———

"But above all, the Loire is light. Its mystery and its secrets appear in its light and the smile on men's faces . . . It has become inseparable from the history of people together, from their trials, their conquests, their works."

Maurice Genevoix

F our kilometers (two and a half miles) north of the construction site, on the left bank of the Loire, lies the fortified village of Saint-Dyé-sur-Loire. It came into being during the seventh century, when the first Christians arrived in the region. They turned it into a place of pilgrimage around the tomb of the hermit Deodatus, whose name was given to the village. In the thirteenth century, it was fortified to protect it from rampant bands of thieves in the region, but only with the building of Chambord, in 1519, did Saint-Dyé truly begin to grow—and grow it did. Lodgings were built for the construction workers, two thousand of whom remained on site as long as their services were

———

The barges docked in the port of Saint-Dyé-sur-Loire.

———

Above: Graffiti of a Loire boat
on a wall of the château of
Chambord.

Facing page:
Saint-Dyé-sur-Loire,
the shores of the Loire,
the last wild river in Europe.

required. Shops and studios opened up, and there were no less than twelve hostelries. Every day, dozens of barges and *gabarres*, the flat boats carrying goods along the Loire, docked on the quays of the port. Among other articles they unloaded the tender and brittle local limestone known as *tuffeau*, for which eleven quarries had been expressly opened in the valley of the Cher (Saint-Aignan, Lye, Belleroche), along with other quarries in closer proximity to Chambord including Marchelin (near Beaugency), Menars and La Chaussée le Comte. An estimated two hundred twenty thousand tons of stone were needed. The slate covering the roofs and adorning the tall chimneys came from Trélazé, close to Angers. The lead used for roofing arrived from England, passing through Rouen by road and river. Oak trunks came down the Loire from Moulins.

A ROYAL
RESIDENCE
IS BUILT

————

"Four leagues from Blois, one league from
the Loire, in a small low-lying valley, amidst muddy
marshland and woods with large oak trees,
far from the nearest roads, out of the blue we
encounter a royal, or rather a magical, château.
One might surmise that bound by some marvelous
lamp, a genie from *One Thousand and
One Nights* had spirited it away from the land of
sunshine and hidden it in the land of fog."

Alfred de Vigny

By 1522 Viart and Sourdeau, who had gotten the project underway, were both dead. The king replaced them with Nicolas de Foyal, who was named superintendent, and Pierre Nepveu (known as Trinqueau), who became master mason. Once the solid foundations had been completed, probably in 1524, the keep, also known as the *donjon* in reference to medieval castles, began to rise; shaped cubically, it was flanked at each angle by an imposing tower. Initially, the sovereign visited the worksite once a year. Each time, he added his own modifications to the original plans, proffered his advice and had no compunctions about motivating the workers with financial enticements. But when he was dissatisfied, he could throw a memorable tantrum.

In February 1525, François I was imprisoned during the Battle of Pavia. Building ground to a halt. His mother acted as regent. Shepherded from one prison to another, he wound up in Madrid. In a 1519 election his rival and jailer, Charles V, the king of Spain, had triumphed over the French sovereign and become the Holy Roman Emperor. On February 21, 1526, following eventful negotiations leading to the Treaty of Madrid, Charles secured François's release. By mid-September, having restored order in the affairs of the kingdom, the monarch returned to Chambord, where he sojourned longer than usual. Building resumed. It was during this period that he decided to reverse existing plans for the north tower of the *donjon*, thereby modifying the

————

The royal cipher of François I
sculpted on the pediment of
a *donjon* window.

————

"Among all the edifices neighboring the town of Blois, the château of Chambord is the most admirable, its model being all but impossible to imitate, given its foundation, its layout and the order in which it was built, which is such that nothing is missing from the perfection required in architecture."

François de Belleforest, 1575

symmetry of the original design and permanently modifying the appearance of the building. He managed teams of masons, stonecutters, carpenters, woodcutters, gardeners, blacksmiths, wheelwrights and roofers. All told, there were more than two thousand persons relaying one another on the worksite! The king then decided to extend the initial project by adding two lateral wings, one for a chapel, and the other as his abode, in addition to a totally enclosed courtyard, thereby endowing the château with its present-day appearance. The *donjon* forms a Greek cross with identically sized branches; at the center, there is the celebrated double helix staircase. Each level is divided into four inhabitable spaces at the extremities of the large cross-shaped room. Four identical dwellings, which can be reached by traversing the large main rooms, cover the squared spaces of the cross, while four other abodes, likewise

identical, are to be found in the corner towers, which can be reached from the loggias opening onto the courtyard. Each of the lodgings contains a large room serving as living space, as well as smaller rooms (oratories, library-studies, cloak-rooms), with a back stairway leading to the mezzanines. When the king was not present, there was little if any furnishing in the dwelling, the reason being that during its numerous peregrinations, the king's court had drapes and carpets and assorted furniture moved out of his previous accommodations, transported and moved into wherever they were sojourning. That much said, the standardized arrangement of forty apartments was highly innovative; in all likelihood, Chambord was the first palace in the history of France to be built as a residential complex. Regardless of their status, when assigned an apartment guests were offered the same degree of comfort. But some

Facing page: The Sologne earth is gorged with water, as we were reminded in June 2016, when the Cosson overflowed its banks.

> **"Yesterday I paid a visit to Chambord. You cannot begin to imagine how singularly beautiful it is. All forms of magic, of poetry and even of *folies* are represented in the admirable peculiarity of this palace of knights and fairies."**
>
> Victor Hugo, 1825

courtiers, wishing to be close enough to the king to receive special treatment, did not hesitate to falsify the door numbers, thereby confusing servants and being awarded the apartment of their choice. Infuriated by these devious maneuvers, a few decades later King Henry III threatened to have the cheaters' hands cut off.

The apartments of François I were an exception to the rule of sameness. Indeed, the sovereign possessed his own apartment in the eastern wing of the château. On the second floor, the four large vaulted rooms of the cross were adorned with more than three hundred coffers sculpted with the emblems of the king: the letter "F" and salamanders. They not only supported the paved terraces on the upper tier, but also concealed a complex rainwater evacuation system. At the top of the terraces, which towered over the woods as far as the eye could see, a fleur-de-lys at a height of 53 meters (174 feet) crowned the lantern tower that prolonged the staircase. One could stroll along the slate roofing of the towers and pavilions and a "forest" of 282 chimneys,

fewer than the legendary 365 chimneys ideally imagined by visitors enthralled by their multitude. By 1537, the lantern towers and the terraces had been completed. In December 1539, wishing to outdo and overawe his permanent rival, the king invited Charles V to Chambord. Together, they went on a stag hunt in the park, after which a celebration with musicians, dancers and comedians was held to honor the emperor, who stayed overnight. Given the occasion, the emperor's room was decorated with gold-embroidered black drapes, and the ceilings were painted with Austrian black eagles. In addition, a featherbed with taffeta covers was set up. Charles visited the castle and was singularly impressed by this architectural wonder and the surrounding opulence: "I see it as a compendium of what human industry can bring into being." In 1545, in what was to be his last stay, the king spent twenty days in Chambord. On March 31, 1547, when he died, a chapel wing and the courtyard enclosure were still under construction, and he would not see his work completed.

Facing page: Top, the carpentry of the Dieudonné tower (west tower of the *donjon*). Bottom, more than two thousand masons, paid piece-rate, relayed one another on the construction site.

Following double-page:
The sculpted panels of the second-floor vaults, with alternations of the monogram of François I and his emblem, the salamander.

"As imperfect as it may remain, Chambord
is one of the miracles of the world."

Pierre de Bourdeille, known as Brantôme, 1570

THE ARCHITECT
KING AND A GENIUS,
LEONARDO DA VINCI

"Details make for perfection, and perfection is not a detail."

Leonardo da Vinci

François I called him "Padre." Leonardo da Vinci and the young monarch met for the first time in Bologna, in the suite of Pope Leo X, following the victory of Marignan in 1515. The year after, when he accepted the invitation of the king and his mother Louise of Savoy to come to France, the master was already sixty-four years old. After his departure from Rome, it took Leonardo four long months to reach the royal court in Amboise. On the back of a mule, he crossed the Alps in the company of his closest student, Francesco Melzi, and Battista de Villanis, his loyal Milanese servant; later in the journey, they would be joined by his long-time companion, Gian Giacomo Caprotti, known as Salai. In the luggage being transported, there were his notebooks and three paintings: *The Virgin and Child with St. Anne*, *St. John the Baptist* and the *Mona Lisa*. François I named Leonardo the "first painter, first engineer and first architect of the king," allotted him a yearly pension of one thousand *écus* and allowed him to stay as long as he wished in the manor of Cloux, presently the château of Clos Lucé, located close to the royal residence of Amboise. The king enjoyed discussions with Leonardo, whom he considered as his mentor. He went so far as to connect the two residences with an underground passage, thereby facilitating informal meetings.

Shortly after his arrival, Leonardo da Vinci went to Romorantin with François I. The king was thinking of converting the centrally located town in Sologne into the new capital of the kingdom. He desired two palaces: one for himself, the other for his mother. This audacious project loomed as an extraordinary challenge for Leonardo, who decided to reconfigure the designs for the ideal city he had imagined being built in Vigevano, near Milan. Retrofitting them to a different environment, he planned to dig canals, to drain the Sologne, to tame the Sauldre and to carve a channel between the Loire and the Saône. He drew up plans for an octagonal pavilion, half circle and half square; his was an extravagant urban project with no equivalent in Europe. Unfortunately, it never saw the light of day; in 1519, a plague epidemic afflicted Romorantin; the same year, Leonardo died; these could have been two good reasons for François I to give up on his idea of a new capital. But the sovereign had no intention of calling it quits; an ardent lover of architecture, he was also out to impress,

Viewed from the sky, the perfectly squared Greek-cross *donjon*, with its four corner towers and its lantern tower in the center.

and still harboring his builder's dream, he chose a site on the shores of the Cosson, Chambord. Much later, during their transfer from Blois to Paris, the archives on the castle's construction were lost, so it is impossible to identify with certainty the architect(s) of the edifice. While some "experts" consulted the documents or examined the models before they were destroyed, their narrations on the paternity of the building remain vague and unconvincing. That much said, the names of the successive project managers have come down to us through account records. As regards the chief architect, while over the centuries historians have more or less plausibly cited several masters—Primaticcio, Vignola, Andrea Palladio, Sebastiano Serlio and Rosso Fiorentino—the most frequently mentioned name is that of Domenico da Cortona, alias "Boccador." A trained carpenter, he is known to have created wood models of the château. Given his relations with Leonardo, it has been hypothesized that following the master's death, Boccador implemented some of his ideas on construction. After all, the two men were well-acquainted and remained in regular touch; moreover, they had jointly contributed to the organization of large-scale court festivities, such as the 1518 wedding of Madeleine de La Tour d'Auvergne and Lorenzo de Medici in Amboise. While superficially persuasive, such considerations do not necessarily justify his being considered as the designer

of Chambord. Exhibiting a surfeit of chauvinism, some past experts heatedly denied the existence of any Italian inspiration. "There is nothing Italian in all that, neither in thought or form," proclaimed the nineteenth-century architect Eugène Viollet-le-Duc, who had stoked controversy with his famed restorations of monuments such as Notre-Dame de Paris. It was only in 1913, however, in a publication by the art historian Marcel Reymond, that the influence of Leonardo in the conception of Chambord began to receive serious attention. Many years after, in the late 1990s, research by archeologists and historians rendered it possible to convincingly underline the imprint left by the old master. During study of his plans and the sketches comprising his codex, numerous similarities have been detected between Leonardo's work and the architecture of Chambord: the centered Greek-cross plan, the multiple flights of stairs, the drainage systems for the roof terraces and the sanitary facilities with air ducts and double-pit latrines. Fascinated by perpetual movement, the ingenious inventor dedicated himself to studies on fluid mechanics and vortex principles. When perusing his plans, the rotational motion of the château is readily apparent. The edifice seems to revolve around the central axis of the staircase and is prolonged toward its summit by the lantern tower, like a helix soaring into the air.

"I would not have traveled so far, had I not deeply desired to see Chambord, where I found that the only person worthy of praising [the château] was he who had it built and who, by his exemplary labor, had achieved perfection calling for admiration."

Marguerite de Navarre, sister of François I

Five centuries later, while an element of mystery endures, it seems obvious that the main creator of the most remarkable Renaissance edifice was none other than its patron: François I himself. Was he guided and inspired in its design by memories of his conversations with Leonardo da Vinci, or was there a previously elaborated project from which the monument's builders little by little diverged, in the absence of the deceased creative genius? What we know for sure is that throughout his reign, François I remained not only highly involved, but totally in charge. Surrounded by artists and intellectuals, during each phase of the project the king was the decision-maker. It was he who selected the ornamentation, rich in symbols, whether in his own or in his mother's image. On May 2, 1519, Leonardo da Vinci died; according to Giorgio Vasari (but the biographer of the master was just seven years old at the time), he expired in the arms of the king; legendary or actual, the scene is represented by Ingres in a celebrated painting; doesn't that represent yet another painterly enigma?

According to the epoch's property law, the estate of a childless foreigner having died in France rightfully belonged to the crown; since Leonardo had obtained letters of naturalization from the sovereign, the rule was not applied. Before dying, the master had designated Francesco Melzi as his testamentary executor. The Amboise public notary never mentioned any painting. As a result, it was to Melzi that Leonardo bequeathed his notes, his sketches and his workshop material. Some of his Tuscany vines were consigned to Battista, and others to Salai, a meager legacy for someone whose relationship with the artist had been long-lasting. That said, during Leonardo's lifetime Salai had already quite possibly drawn his share. In 1518, before returning to Italy, the artist entrusted his disciple with his paintings. Not willing to entertain the thought of their leaving France, the king bought three of them, including the *Mona Lisa*. The most emblematic Renaissance painting was initially transported to Fontainebleau, and then to the Louvre. More than four centuries later, when Nazi Germany was menacing France, the national museum collections were evacuated. At first, in 1938, the *Mona Lisa* was to be found in a nondescript wooden crate bearing the simple inscription LP0 (Louvre Painting and the number 0) and three red discs denoting the importance of its contents. It was then conveyed to Chambord, where for close to a month, it remained hidden in the chapel broom closet. Following what turned out to be a false alarm, it was brought back to the Louvre, but on June 3 and June 4, 1940, just ten days before the Nazis entered Paris, prior to being ferried to safety in the south of France, where it remained until the end of the war, it transited through the château. By a curious turn of events, had the *Mona Lisa* come back to admire the work of her creator, the genius?

"Chambord is a monument of beauty and intelligence. Chambord is the very expression of the Renaissance. At once royal palace, hunting lodge and evocation of the ideal city of heavenly Jerusalem, the château conveys such enduring architectural strength that none of the rulers subsequent to François I dared modify its envelope of stone."

Jean d'Haussonville

MAGICAL AND FASCINATING,
THE STAIRCASE SOARS TO THE SKY

———

"Chambord has a single double staircase, to descend and ascend without being seen: an ideal setting for the mysteries of war and love."

François-René de Chateaubriand

"Monsieur preceded me to Chambord, which is three leagues (ten miles) from Blois: it is his castle, built by François I in a highly extraordinary maner ... One of the most curious and remarkable aspects of the house consists of the steps [the grand staircase], which are arranged in such a way that one person can go up and a second go down without their ever meeting, even though they can see one another: that was how Monsieur took pleasure as he started playing with me. When I arrived, he was at the top of the staircase; then he descended as I ascended, and laughed loudly to see me running, as I was thinking I'd catch up to him. I was thrilled over the pleasure he was taking, and even more thrilled once I had joined him."
"La Grande Mademoiselle," the ten-year-old daughter of Gaston, duke of Orléans, 1637

Its two ramps in spirals nested one above the other around a hollow column appear to merge, but they never meet. The monumental double revolution or double helix staircase remains as fascinating as ever. At the very center of the *donjon*, it reaches each floor and rises up, all the way to the terraces, where its ascension toward the sky culminates in the lantern tower. People can go up or down without ever meeting, its apertures enabling them to catch a glimpse of those using the ramp opposite. Located above the empty core of the tower, a narrow staircase goes up to the summit and leads to a final landing, that of the lantern, with its walls completely covered by clear and stained glass. The staircase is an architectural marvel. It embodies the perfect harmony of the proportions of the building taken as a whole. Its stone helix seems to turn on an axis as it takes flight, like a dizzying transcription of the studies on the principles of universal dynamics carried forward by the engineering genius. Indeed, in Leonardo's notebooks, there exists a design for a multiflight staircase (*Manuscript B*, conserved in the Bibliothèque de l'Institut de France).

Splendid works of art, two hundred capitals surmount the pilasters underscoring the double ascension. The whole staircase is adorned with lush, finely engraved backgrounds illustrating the oppositions and antagonisms between good and evil, vice and virtue: angels and satyrs, masks, fantastic creatures, cornucopias, foliage, cabinets, and so forth. On the ground floor, at the bottom of the staircase, one of the pillar's capitals contains a simple, unobtrusive triangle pointing downwards, representing the three nails of the Passion of Christ and constituting a symbol of the Trinity in religious art. For its designer, the Chambord staircase may have been the pathway ascending toward God.

Above: The lantern overlooking the staircase.

Facing page: The staircase viewed from the second floor.

Following pages: Left, inside the double helix staircase. Right, inside the lantern tower summit.

WELL-CARVED
SECRETS

—

"Nutrisco et extinguo"
(I nourish myself with the good fire,
and I extinguish the bad)

The motto of François I

C hambord is a mystery. Ever since its creation, the choice of its location, the absence of any known and acknowledged architect, the disappearance of the archives, the supposed influence of Leonardo da Vinci and its ornamentation with its occult symbols have led to numerous theories and speculations, some of them earnest and others quirky, on their inter–pretation. For example, there is no escaping the salamander, an amphibious creature found in the wetlands of Sologne. Considered during the Middle Ages as a magic and legendary animal, it thrives on land and in water alike, and has been credited with the power to withstand flames. It had been the emblem of François's grandfather, John, count of Angoulême, whose commitment to reconciliation averted turmoil in the kingdom and won him comparison with a salamander putting out fires. For his tenth birthday, the young king was given a medallion showcasing the animal. Offered by his mother, Louise of Savoy, it bore an inscription engraved in Italian: "Notrisco al buono stingo el reo" (I nourish myself with the good fire, and I extinguish the bad), which had been adopted by his tutor, François de Moulins

de Rochefort. Inspiration was undoubtedly drawn from a work published in 1499 and celebrated in its times, *Dream of Poliphilus,* by the Venetian monk Francesco Colonna: "The salamander is seen as a symbol of temperance, and the prince was asked to draw sustenance from the fire of love for wisdom while steering clear of the destructive fires of turbulent passion, unworthy of a prince." A symbol of peace which is said to extinguish the fires of war while feeding itself with spiritual fire, the salamander, with an abridged version of the Latin motto "Nutrisco et extinguo," became the symbol of François I once he acceded to the throne. It may be found at hundreds of locations within the edifice, sculpted in wood or carved in stone. In the immense vaults of the second floor of the *donjon,* it alternates with François's "F" monogram, embellished with heraldic Franciscan Savoy knots, the familial emblem of the king's mother symbolizing the protection afforded by Saint Francis of Paola and Saint Francis of Assisi. Each coffer, animal or letter is sculpted differently; out of the 150 "F" let–ters, only one has been inverted, for no apparent reason. On the ceiling of the central staircase, on the other hand, all of the monograms are inverted:

why so? According to some commentators, by heavenly pathways they are addressed to God, the Lord alone being able to read them in the right order. According to others, they represent a homage to Leonardo, who wrote backwards (to decipher his codices, a mirror is necessary). Be that as it may! As a coded, encrypted, secretive palace, Chambord does not readily allow the visitor to lift the veil of mystery desired by its creator. Historians, archeologists, researchers and dreamers have all conducted investigations of its unique, futurist structure with its formal geometry corresponding to a square or Greek cross-shaped plan in which symmetry is established around the central staircase, endowing it with a gyratory sense that has no known architectural equivalent,

a transposition of stone in a rotational movement bespeaking the research of Leonardo. Chambord may also be viewed as an interpretation of heavenly Jerusalem: an ideal city in which justice and fraternity would reign, as described in the Apocalypse of St. John the Apostle, with its four towers lined up with the four cardinal points, twelve doors in groups of three on each side of the *donjon* (they once actually existed, their hinges remain visible), square plan, absence of any apparent chancel, luminosity and cherubs that populate the chimneys and the dormers, like the watchmen portrayed in the Bible. While many of the mottos, monograms and salamanders are easily understandable, other more enigmatic emblems throughout the château remain hidden. François I was keenly interested in the

Facing page: Carved capital atop the lantern tower.

Right: Top, all the monograms on the ceiling around the lantern have been inverted. Bottom, amidst the hundreds of monograms and salamanders adorning the second-floor ceiling, only one is mysteriously sculpted backwards.

occult sciences. In 1519, it was from the Franciscan monk Jean Thenaud, whom he had frequented since his childhood and who was appreciated for many years by the king's mother, Louise of Savoy, that he ordered a work in French explaining the Christian kabbalah, in which the essential dogmas of Christianity were rumored to be found. Far from motivated by the idea, the monk hesitated before complying with the king's request by providing him with a prose version of the *Traité de la cabale*, which ended with a warning on the dangers of magical and kabbalistic practices. The influence of the monk and his writings undeniably weighed on François's choices of emblems for Chambord. These symbols, which were earmarked for those who could decipher them, deliver a kind of second architectural reading. They include large numbers of crowns (closed as an imperial symbol, or circularly open), fleur-de-lys, porcupines, heartbroken swans, geometrical figures and the royal cipher, King François's personal emblem.

During the eighteenth century the count of Saint-Germain, a peculiar character, a highly cultivated smooth-talking adventurer, was an intriguing figure in Parisian salons. Nothing was known about his birth or background. He fancied himself several centuries old, claimed to possess the secrets of immortality and also boasted, due to his research as an alchemist, of being able to manufacture precious stones. Casanova recounts how Saint-Germain had turned a copper coin into gold. The marquess of Pompadour, the king's mistress, introduced him to Louis XV. The sovereign was in possession of a blemished diamond; one month later, Saint-Germain gave back a strikingly pure stone, and said he was close to holding the secret of the philosopher's stone. Utterly won over, the king asked the marquess of Marigny, director general of the king's buildings, to place the château of Chambord at the disposal of the count for pursuit of his alchemical quests. In 1758, along with his assistants, he settled into the castle, and got down to work in his laboratory. He devised and fine-tuned colored glass, manufactured synthetic gemstones, and developed new dyes for painting, only to be accused of espionage and compelled to leave France. A charlatan, illusionist or honest-to-goodness discoverer, he remains a mystery. Over the ensuing centuries and even relatively recently, people have reported crossing paths with the immortal count of Saint-Germain!

In our time, with minimal historical or scientific rigor and a panoply of complex mathematical calculations, a number of highly problematical conclusions have been drawn on the building of Chambord: concordance with the Egyptian pyramids, secret codes, hidden plans pointing to a royal axis between Chambord and Fontainebleau or concealed messages. To this day, observation of the château kindles the imagination and generates surprising theories. The multiple squares forming the plan of the castle become an alphabet given voice as a game of hidden words. Even more astoundingly, the helical staircase is said to resemble a DNA molecule, while the summit of the lantern tower would be akin to a rocket ready to be launched heavenward.

Left: Two details of
the capitals adorning
the double helix staircase.

Right: Top, the triangle of
the Holy Trinity at the
entrance to the double helix
staircase. Bottom, the final
year of construction work is
engraved on the terrace
and the lantern tower.

Following pages: Details of
the roof ornaments.

HUNTING,
FIVE CENTURIES OF TRADITION

——

"Aged and ailing, I will have myself carried to the hunt, and when dead, I will perhaps wish to go there in my coffin."

François I

During the Renaissance, under François I, hunting with hounds, or *vénerie*, became an art of living. Considered the "Father of the Hunters," the king shared his passion on horseback, and also practiced game bird hunting, or falconry, with specially trained raptors. In 1545, some 150 falconers and 300 birds of prey were doing the king's bidding. After the French Revolution, starting in 1789, hunting was democratized. While some bow or bird hunting is still occasionally organized on the estate, the last *vénerie* dates back to March 1947. It was the French academician Maurice Druon, author of "Chant des partisans," who had the honor of the last ritual severing of a stag foreshank in the history of Chambord: "As a young and humble hunter, in Chambord I carried out a tradition that had lasted four centuries." That year, the estate became a national wildlife reserve.

——

Facing page: Stag trophy in the château hunting room.
Following pages: Three ways of hunting—with a gun, a bow and in flight (falconer).

——

Above: Bow hunting.

Facing page: During a regulated hunting party (*battue*), the hunters are anchor points, while the trackers run the animals down.

Over recent decades, hunting parties have been transformed into regulatory game hunts. Without predators, the balance of nature in the estate would be jeopardized. To ensure equilibrium and avoid animal overpopulation in a hermetically closed forest, each year a third of the animals needs to be removed. A hunting day is always marked by scrupulous observation of the selfsame ritual. Early in the morning the guests gather together in the *salle des Chasses* on the ground floor of the château, a room decorated with gilded gold leaf trophies and impressive paintings depicting legendary hunting scenes. In full dress, forestry officials inspect participants' hunting permits and provide instructions for the day. The hunters embark in estate vehicles taking them to preliminarily designated areas. In the underbrush, the inaugural horn resounds, and a hundred trackers tumultuously move forward; shots reverberate, animals fall. Lunch is served beside a pond at *La Thibaudière*, a wooden pavilion built at the request of Georges Pompidou, and then the hunt resumes. In the evening, close to the château on the Avenue du Roi in the glow of braziers, honors are rendered to the game exhibited on a bed of foliage. Trackers and hunters gather together near the hunting bag; on horseback, swords drawn, the Republican Guards present their arms and the horns of Chambord resound. The commanding officer, the hunting leader, addresses the assembly with a solemn ceremonial speech, conveying his thanks to trackers and estate staff alike. Before the hunters, he indicates the number of shots fired and animals downed; lastly he greets and commends each one of the participants.

Below: Forest officers verify hunting licenses and give instructions for the day.

Facing page: Bottom, lunch at the La Guillonnière farm.

84

In the evening, in front of
the hunting bag, honors
are bestowed on the game
by the cavalrymen of
the Republican Guard and
the Chambord Ecole de
trompe (hunting horn school).

FROM
THE ROYAL
CAPTAINCY
TO THE
REPUBLICAN
GUARD

**"The safeguard and conservation of the woods
and bushes, the red and black quarry of this park,
for our pleasure and pastime or pursuit of game."**

François I, 1542

In 1516, François I proceeded to the regulation of hunting rights. Only the king and his nobles would be allowed to hunt. And yet, poaching persisted. To put an end to it, in 1542 the king created royal captaincies, which were tasked with ensuring "the safeguard and conservation of the woods and bushes, the red and black quarry of this park, for our pleasure and pastime or pursuit of game." Hunting in the estate of Chambord was placed under the authority of a captain and three guards. The captains all too frequently committed abuses on the local population, and their tarnished reputation led to their disappearance in 1777 under Louis XVI. After the French Revolution abolished aristocratic privilege, democratized hunting rights jeopardized the ecosystem; that is one reason why Napoleon I introduced hunting licenses. As the price of a license was equivalent to one month of a farmer's salary, hunting once again became a privileged activity for the fortunate few. In our times, hunting is regulated, and only those having passed a test have the right to carry and use firearms.

The château stables.

In 1970, President Georges Pompidou designated Chambord as big game presidential hunting land. In 1972 the Republican Guard, which reports to the gendarmerie and is responsible for the safety of the presidency of the French Republic and the security of the national monuments, moved into the château, where a permanent mounted police station was set up, rooms and stables included. Three Republican Guards and nine gendarmes were tasked with providing surveillance and maintaining the security of the château, the village and the forested areas in partnership with the police of the ONCFS (the national agency for hunting and wildlife). Up until the early twentieth century the six doors (today there are five) of the wall surrounding the estate were closed at night to keep poachers out. Even though today's poachers are few and far between, a territory as extensive as Paris needs to be kept under the vigilance of gendarmes on horseback patrol. Only one-fifth of the estate is open to the public, the remaining four-fifths are of restricted access: a protected reserve.

Facing page: Every day, gendarmes of the Chambord mounted police station monitor the estate, the areas open to the public as well as the reserve.

Following double-page: The farrier of the Republican Guard in the château stables.

LOVE LIFE
IN CHAMBORD,
KISS AND TELL

"Women are versatile, in no way reliable."

François I, according to Brantôme

François I was a handsome, distinguished and cultivated man who embodied power not only on account of his title, but also due to his prominent physical stature and unusual vitality. He enjoyed the company of women. When he explored the lands of Chambord and Montfrault with his "small gang" in tow, the young king and his hunting companions were invariably accompanied by courtesans. François was married twice. His first wife was Claude de France, who died in childbirth at the age of twenty-five, after having given the sovereign some seven children over nine years. His second wife was Eleanor of Austria, sister of Charles V, the victorious Holy Roman Emperor who during negotiations of the Treaty of Madrid made the marriage one of the conditions to be fulfilled before the French sovereign could be released from jail. Their engagement was contracted by proxy on January 21, 1526. Back in France, however, François denounced the treaty, and it was only after conclusion of a new pact, "The Ladies' Peace," which was signed in Cambrai in 1529, that their wedding finally took place, on July 7, 1530, in a small church in southwestern France, without pomp and ceremony. The marriage was destined to remain a sterile one. On the other hand, the chivalrous prince who once proclaimed that "a court without women is like a flowerless garden" is generally credited with a large number of mistresses. While no document relates the sovereign's intimate personal life, the amorous legend was kept enduringly alive; the myth was perpetuated by novelistic historians who revisited the sixteenth century according to the moods of their times. Officially, only two mistresses have been attributed to the ruler. The first was Françoise de Foix, countess of Châteaubriant, who dwelt in Brittany at her husband's side. Her renowned beauty and intelligence drew the sovereign's attention. At first she became the queen's lady-in-waiting; only in 1516 did she let her royal suitor have his way. And the second? Back from captivity, François was introduced to Anne de Pisseleu, duchess of Étampes, an attractive eighteen-year-old blonde with whom he promptly fell head over heels. Wishing to remain in favor with the king, for two years the two women fought tooth and nail against one another. Anne prevailed and kept François company until his last breath. As for his other alleged mistresses, the suppositions are devoid of historical foundation. For example, Marie Gaudin, so-called "Dame de la Bourdaisière," was reputed to have been the most beautiful woman in the kingdom and to have become the king's initial mistress. Then there was Marie Boleyn, about whom the sovereign is said to have remarked following their separation that she was "a major league slut, the most nefarious of all."

Graffiti on a château wall.

Not to mention Claude de Rohan-Gié, countess of Thoury, for whose sake the king was rumored to have expanded Chambord in 1540, and "La Belle Ferronière," whose jealous husband was allegedly so determined to avenge her idyll with the monarch as to transmit the syphilis bacteria so as to contaminate his errant wife and her royal lover, thereby doing away with the two of them.

When it came to trysts, Chambord bore witness to far more than the occasional *amours* of its creator. If the walls could speak, they would have many additional lovers' secrets to reveal. For example, when King Henri II came to Chambord, he was accompanied by Queen Catherine de' Medici . . . and also by his mistress, Diane of Poitiers, who was accommodated not in the château, but rather in the Montmorency hotel now known as "Lina's Farm," located but one hundred yards away, on the southern lawn. As stealthily as he could, Henri appeared there every night. However, a piece of Diane's heart belonged to another lover, Maréchal de Brissac. One evening, as they were making passionate love and had become blissfully unaware of what time it was, Brissac came to his senses and flew the coop, just before the arrival of the king. In his precipitate flight, he was discovered by the Grand Master of Artillery Claude de Taïs, who made fun of him. Feeling offended, Brissac complained to his mistress. The king removed de Taïs and had him replaced . . . by Diane's lover. He still knew nothing of the clandestine adventures of the

dame he adored. Out of love for the two women, he had his roofing adorned with the initials of his wife and those of his mistress.

A century later Louis XIII took Anne of Austria to Chambord for their honeymoon. During a dinner in the château he came upon Mademoiselle de Hautefort, with whom he fell in platonic love, hiding a note in her bodice. Curious but shy, Louis XIII did not dare place his fingers inside the garment. Having developed a bond with the maiden, his wife demanded that he ferret it out. The sovereign obeyed by taking a pair of silver tweezers to retrieve the paper, as the two ladies looked on amusedly. It was a letter mocking the way the King appeared to favor the maiden . . .

Louis XIV often came to Chambord, where he undertook multiple renovations with improving comfort in mind. He also organized sumptuous festivities, always in the company of his favorites: Marie Mancini, Françoise-Louise de La Vallière, the marquesses of Maintenon and Montespan. It was in a room at the château that one of the king's cousins, Anne-Marie-Louise d'Orléans, Mademoiselle de Montpensier, also known as "La Grande Mademoiselle," declared her passion for the duke of Lauzun. After blowing onto a mirror, she sketched his name with her finger on its foggy surface.

Under Louis XV, Maurice the count of Saxony, who cherished hunting as much as he adored women (and vice versa), came to live in the château. A hardened bachelor, he had one affair after another. He organized spectacles for

On the château terraces.

"A court without women is like a flowerless garden."

François I

she was locked up in a convent. She finally gave in to Maurice's harassment and moved into the château to be with him. Legend has it that his final liaison, with the princess of Conti, occasioned his death. As a dishonored husband, the prince may have sought redress, challenging the count to a duel and mortally wounding him. According to some, it was the other way around: the count slew the prince. In reality, Maurice lost his life after having caught a cold, which was abysmally treated.

While Chambord subsequently grew older and wiser, its romanticism, its mystery and its poetry continued to appeal to the hearts of artists as well as lovers. As an ideal city, it had been taken by Rabelais as a model for his Abbey of Thélème. Centuries later, it likewise inspired Alfred de Vigny, who compared it to a palace from *One Thousand and One Nights*. And as a fairy tale castle, it became the décor for *Peau d'âne* (*Donkey Skin*), the 1970 movie directed by Jacques Demy and co-starring Catherine Deneuve, Jacques Perrin and Jean Marais. From their hearts engraved in the *tuffeau* limestone and their hide-and-seek games in the staircase to their tender kisses on the terraces, lovers are perpetually present in Chambord, some of them coming from around the world to immortalize their couple.

his guests, and had a theater set up on the second floor, to which he invited a multitude of young and attractive actresses. With one of his mistresses, a young opera singer named Marie-Geneviève Rinteau, he had a daughter, who was to become the grandmother of George Sand. With the actor Favart's wife, matters were more complicated. At first, Mademoiselle de Chantilly would not surrender to Maurice, whose response consisted of obtaining a *lettre de cachet* from the king forcing her husband to take flight; in the meantime,

CHAMBORD OVER TIME:
ROYAL THEATER, A MARÉCHAL'S GARRISON OR PRINCIPALITY

———

"I am altogether content with your comedy, here is the truly comic and the fine and useful joke."

Louis XIV to Molière, October 1670 in Chambord

Following the death of François I, his son Henry II showed lessened interest in Chambord but pursued ongoing work projects; the walls of the chapel planned by his father were erected. But when he died tragically, in a jousting tournament in Paris in 1559, the chapel remained unfinished and his widow, Catherine de' Medici, evinced little or no interest in the château, preferring to "read" the future by staring into the stars from the top of the lantern tower. The year after, their son François II passed away. And while Charles IX came from time to time to hunt, his successors, Henry III and Henry IV, never did. Only in 1610, with the reign of Louis XIII, did another king honor the estate with his presence. In 1626, he granted château prerogatives to his brother Gaston, duke of Orleans, who was placed under house arrest there in 1634. Having been abandoned for too many years and decades, the edifice was subject to water ingress and excessive

humidity. It was Gaston who initiated long-overdue restoration; he began to waterproof the terraces and repaired the casings on the second floor and in the lantern tower. In 1659, Louis XIV discovered Chambord. A year later, back from Fontarabie following his wedding with Maria Theresa of Spain, he returned to the château, which he particularly appreciated during the *brame* (deer mating season). Starting in 1668, he showed up for three consecutive years, but due to his preference for the comforts of Versailles, for over a decade he steered clear of the Cosson shores, to which he finally returned three times, in 1682, 1684 and 1685. However, his on-and-off presence did not prevent him from initiating major and costly projects, the first of which got underway in 1664. Outside, he had a pheasantry developed at the present-day location of the Maison des Réfractaires, had the park walls repaired, and had built not only the Saint-Louis parish church,

A bust of Molière on the first floor of the château, where he presented *Le Bourgeois gentilhomme* in a world premiere.

———

Left: The ceremonial bedchamber. Installed by Louis XIV around 1680, in 1748 it was redecorated by Maurice, count of Saxony.

Facing page: The governor's bedchamber, installed by the marquess of Polignac in 1786.

but also a presbytery on today's Place Saint-Michel, not to mention a stable containing three hundred horses. In addition, he asked his architect Jules Hardouin-Mansart to complete unfinished work in the chapel. Having remained without a roof, for over a century it had been getting wetter and wetter. Located in the western tower, the nave with its immense upraised vault intruded on the structure, compelling the architect to engage in resourceful carpentry to maintain the external appearance of the château, of which the nave finally became the largest room. In the forecourt, Hardouin-Mansart completed the pantries commenced under Henry II and covered the wings of the roof, which no longer exists today. That said, the type of roofing owes its

name—a mansard roof, also known in English as a curb roof or garret—to the renowned architect. In parallel, the castle interior was rearranged to accommodate the thousands of courtiers accompanying the king. With the exception of the royal apartments, it was partitioned into small lodgings. The first floor featured the king's chamber, the guard room, a billiard area and a theater. It was there, on October 14, 1670, that Molière presented the grand premiere of *Le Bourgeois gentilhomme*, which was supposed to ridicule the Turks. The play had been commissioned by the king, who wished to avenge the scornful behavior of the "Grand Turk" ambassador during a party organized in his honor the year before. With the monarch seated in the audience,

Molière scathingly satirized the bourgeoisie of his time. In the play Monsieur Jourdain, a moneyed parvenu wishing to become a man of quality and be ennobled, refused to give his daughter away to the man she loved, claiming that he was no *gentil-homme*. But when the young man introduced himself as the son of the "Grand Turk" and proposed, in exchange for the hand of his daughter, to honor him with the title of "Grand Mamamouchi," he changed his mind and came around. An Oriental dance closed the play, with music by Lully in the background. As the king failed to applaud, the courtiers who had disapproved of the production rejoiced. But five days later, the king requested that it be given again: "I did not talk to you about your play after the first performance, but in all honesty you had never previously done anything I found more entertaining, and your play is excellent. . . . Here is the truly comic and the fine and useful joke; keep on working in this style, you will be giving me pleasure." Molière's twenty-fifth play was a resounding success that propelled him to the height of his glory. Back in the château, each sojourn of the Sun King was an occasion for sumptuous festivities, theatrical performances, concerts, fireworks, banquets and hunting parties. In 1715, Louis XV succeeded his great-grandfather. From 1725 to 1733, he organized the stay in Chambord of his father-in-law Stanislas Leszczyński, exiled king of Poland. For the sake of his comfort, furniture was brought in from Paris and Marly, while drainage of the Cosson River and landscaping of the formal gardens were completed. On August 25, 1745, Louis XV conferred the château to Maurice de Saxe for life as a reward for his military exploits, particularly his victory in the Battle of Fontenoy. The maréchal resided there in the company of his court and his light cavalry regiment. Military order reigned in Chambord, where one thousand men in the Saxe-Volontaires regiment were quartered starting in May 1749. It was divided into six brigades, of which the first was the "Colonelle" or the "White," according to the color of its horses, the soldiers' helmet flaps and their flags. It was the maréchal's personal Republican Guard; a major

singularity, unprecedented at the time, consisted in its being composed exclusively of "people of color" from the African continent, from Madagascar, from Pondicherry, from Cayenne or from the West Indies; their uniforms were adorned with panther or sheep skins and bordered with red fabric. The Guard was directed by a former cook from Guinea, Jean Hitton. Every Sunday the maréchal, who was in fact a Lutheran, led his men to Mass under the perplexed and occasionally worried eyes of the population; that said, a few mixed-race births were recorded. The other brigades were formed by Uhlan cavaliers from throughout Europe. With their shaved heads and profuse moustaches, they rode horses harnessed as in Hungary. Discipline was de rigueur, with daily military reviews and reception of guests to the sound of the six cannons placed at the château entrance. The maréchal reigned over the estate like a king, and he rendered justice; according to the gravity of the offense, the offender was given a reprimand or sent to prison; capital punishment was not unheard of. Two public executions took place, one of an Uhlan (for repeated desertion), the other of a "dragon" (for the rape of a shepherdess); both of them were hanged in public from an elm tree on the main square. On another score, the maréchal instigated projects in the park and built new roads to facilitate hunting. He transformed the stables into barracks, set up a small theater, modernized the royal apartment by having it redecorated and put the finishing touches on the formal French gardens. On November 30, 1750, Maurice died in the château, which

Previous double-page: The trophy room adjoins the west wing of the château on the second floor.

Facing page: The château chapel, completed by the architect Jules Hardoin Mansart at the request of Louis XIV.

was inherited by his nephew, the count of Friesen. What he did not inherit was his uncle's passion for Chambord, and he turned over the estate to farmers. The building controller observed its pitiable state and reported his findings to his superiors; shortly afterwards, the château reverted to the French crown. In 1782, the marquess of Polignac took possession of the property, but during the French Revolution, he abandoned the castle, which was overrun by villagers and poachers who reveled in the temporary lawlessness of the place. The wall was breached and pierced, the larger animals decimated, the trees cut down. Troops were sent in to restore order, but they did not succeed. If the furniture had not been plundered, it was auctioned off, and the doors and windows, as well as anything else that could be sold, were wantonly vandalized. There was even talk of putting the castle up for sale.

But in 1790 René-Honoré Marie, the former chief building inspector, came to the defense of Chambord by demonstrating the unusual patrimonial interest of the edifice; moreover, he managed to convince the public authorities that "light maintenance" would suffice to ensure its conservation. In August 1793 the municipality of Chambord, which was compelled in accordance with republican law to do away with all royal emblems, appointed two expert appraisers. Stock-taking was so successful that, following their evaluation of the daunting task lying ahead and of its humongous cost, only the church was forced to withdraw its furnishings and accoutrements redolent of the *Ancien Régime*. So it is that Chambord was one of the rare French castles to have conserved its royal ornamentations. In 1805, Napoleon expressed the wish to set up an institute for the education of the daughters of *Légion*

113

d'Honneur awardees in the castle, but the project never got off the ground. On August 15, 1809 the emperor granted the estate along with an annuity of five hundred thousand francs to Maréchal Berthier as a reward for his work as long-time chief of staff. Chambord was renamed Principality of Wagram but remained state property. Berthier enjoyed a right to habitation (usufruct), and had to maintain not just the edifice, but the estate in its entirety. It was in his absence, however, that farm restoration was organized and merino sheep breeding began; the château, on the other hand, underwent neglect. And only once, in 1810 for a hunting party, did Berthier actually stay in Chambord. Never having made himself at home on the estate, in 1815 he died. The château was in a sorry state and, standing in need of money, his widow sought permission to sell it off. In 1821, the estate was acquired following a national fundraising campaign and given to Henri d'Artois, duke of Bordeaux and grandson of King Charles X. The Revolution of 1830 forced his grandfather to abdicate in favor of Henri, but on August 9, Louis-Philippe of Orléans was proclaimed king of France. As an adult, having become Henri, count of Chambord, it was from his different European residences that he administered his château, with which he had little or no familiarity. In 1870, Napoleon III capitulated subsequent to the defeat of the French by the Prussians. The following year, legislative elections were held, and the royalists prevailed largely, winning twice as many seats as the republicans; what a godsend for partisans of the restoration of monarchy in France! But royalists were a house divided against itself: on the one hand, the partisans of the Maison d'Orléans; on the other hand, the Legitimists (the Bourbons) headed by Henri, who returned to France and set foot in Chambord for the first time on July 4, 1871, at the age of fifty-one. He stayed there for a few days, just enough time to draft his manifesto, in which he laid emphasis on principles drawn from the *Ancien Régime* and emphasized his undying attachment to the traditional white flag, which he steadfastly refused to give up in favor of the tricolor flag, which

he deemed an unacceptable symbol of revolution: "I will not allow the banner of Henri IV, of François I and of Joan of Arc to be wrested from my hands." Prior to going back into exile, he ordered a royal carriage to eventually bring him back to Paris. And even though the two sides finally agreed to a compromise solution, on October 30, 1873 a letter from the count was published in the daily paper *L'Union*, in which he declined to accept the crown. Not wishing to be the king legitimizing the revolution (the tricolor would have remained the national flag, while the white fleur-de-lys would have been the monarchy's standard), he refused to give ground in his advocacy of the traditional white flag. Had his stubbornness paved the way to defeat? Was he using the flag as a pretext? Or was he exhibiting pride fueled by steadfast determination? Was he a man of honor, or a single-minded, if not simple-minded, fool? None of these explanations can be totally ruled out. Some might mockingly claim that by declining the throne, he was an inadvertent founder of the Republic. In any event, there would be no Henry V—and there would be no more French monarchy, period. There would never be another king, neither in France, nor in Chambord, even if, up until 1914, on every January 21 the school in Chambord was closed to commemorate the death of Louis XVI, and the schoolchildren attended a Remembrance mass.

Music, theater and prodigious celebrations have immemorially punctuated life in the château.

HISTORY INSCRIBED
ON THE WALLS

"I engraved my name at the apex
of the highest tower."

Victor Hugo, 1825

Tuffeau, the tender and fragile limestone from which the castle is built, has always provided celebrated and anonymous visitors alike, not to mention today's at-times indelicate tourists, with an opportunity to leave an imprint of their stay in Chambord. Over the centuries, they have engraved thousands of graffiti. Ever since its construction, with the markings of the workers, and later on, long before the monument was opened to the public, with those made by the occupants and their guests, "signatures" have always abounded. The first of these were stonecutters'; they are craftsmen's testimonials, composed of simple geometric forms, of overlapping triangles, of the letters of the alphabet, of circles and of arrows. They afford proof of the work of laborers paid piece-rate.

Graffiti on the château terraces.

Facing page: a 17th-century drawing in the château's cupbearers'room. **Right:** Graffiti inside the château: souvenirs of the shooting of *Peau d'âne*, signatures of Victor Hugo and Jean de La Fontaine.

Other marks, more elementary and resembling Roman numerals, were used by masons to ensure the correct positioning of stone blocks. There are volutes or minimalist plans, such as sketches engraved to memorize the work to be done before cutting, or blueprints on blocks for which the placement was modified as work proceeded. And then there are mariners' memories, with sketches of boats on the Loire. Of less benefit to the edifice and impossible to count are the number of lovers' hearts, of philosophical meditations, or of signatures from the hands of unknown or distinguished figures such as Jean de La Fontaine in 1653 or Victor Hugo in 1825. The latter wished to leave an imprint of his passage by inscribing his name, and he even owned up, in a letter to his friend Paul Saint-Valéry, to having stolen away with a chunk of stone and moss, and a piece of wood engraved by none other than François I. On a doorway, we can read an inscription recalling the shooting by Jacques Demy, in 1970, of *Peau d'âne*; in a staircase, another inscription is due to the Blois firemen who, in 1945, quelled a fire threatening to engulf the edifice. A small part of the château served as the cupbearers' room; that was where the king's officers and the attendants tasked with wine opening and serving came to store silverware and bottles of the finest *grands crus*. The cupbearers of Gaston, duke of Orléans and his wife Marguerite covered the walls with numerous charcoal drawings: a depiction of a huge buffet table with its plates, its cups and its goblets (what better way to memorize a table setting plan?), an impressive salamander above a door, a globe in which Europe and Africa may be divined and an imaginary castle.

During excavation in the pit latrines, signs were discovered: marks made by the stonecutters during construction. And then, beneath the northern tower, in the cesspit of the royal wing, there were these surprising poems written in 1845 by a manservant:

"Seuls en ces lieux aimant la solitude
Nous profitons d'un moment de loisir
Pour livrer nos cœurs comme à notre habitude
À leurs réflections, tel est notre seul plaisir."
(*Alone in these places adoring solitude,*
We relish a moment of rest,
To give our hearts over as usual
To their reflections, that is our single
pleasure.)

But the most mysterious and enigmatic of the graffiti is the one that Brantôme recalls having espied in the late sixteenth century, beside the window of the royal chamber, in the handwriting of François I: "Women are versatile." A century later, the physician Jean Bernier claimed to have read on the window pane of a cabinet abutting the castle chapel: "Souvent femme varie, Mal habil qui s'y fie" (women often change their minds, it makes no sense to rely on their word). Is this the masonry that Victor Hugo stole away with? A writer's fantasy, a forgery . . . There is no way of verifying the authenticity of the quotation or the existence of the inscription. In the collective imagination, François I remains the most renowned "graffiti scribbler" of Chambord.

Charcoal drawings in the cupbearers' room of the château.

THE LEGEND OF THE "BLACK HUNTER" IN THE MONTFRAULT PAVILION

"When a fearful resident of Sologne, having walked on the grass that leads astray, finds himself towards midnight near the pavilion of Montfrault, he is liable to encounter the frightening figure of a hunter who is none other than Thibault the Trickster . . . , first hereditary count of Blois. Showing up late for Mass at the church of Thoury, the priest having refrained from delaying the service to await his arrival, Thibault expressed his discontent by slaying the officiant. In punishment for his crimes, after his death divine anger forced him to vainly pursue the same stag, forevermore"; that is what the legend relates. It is he who can be heard departing, during pleasant autumn evenings, in a clamorous movement of men, horses, dogs and horns signaling a hunting party soaring through the air without ever being seen. Montfrault is located southeast of the estate.

By the eighteenth century, its castle had fallen into utter disrepair, and it was decided to raze what was left of it, and use the stone to construct a stud farm. Today, just a few walls survive, as has a moss-covered vaulted cave with its ancient staircase sinking ever more deeply into the earth in the midst of a wooded area. Once again using the stones of the demolished edifice, a new pavilion was built for the guards, who up until then had resided in the two remaining inhabitable rooms of the château. While today the gates of the Montfrault pavilion are locked and it is no longer a benchmark on the road to Chambord, from the forest of Boulogne near the pond of Montperché, the building may yet be perceived from across the grates. It is used as a residence by the chief forestry officer of the estate, who cohabits with the legendary "Black Hunter."

Cellar of the ancient château
of Montfrault.

"To vainly pursue the same stag, forevermore."

THE RENAISSANCE
OF THE GARDENS

"Placed on a terrace that forms a pedestal, the gardens not only offer a promenade, but also serve as a monument. They highlight its foundations, its perspectives, its dimensions"

Jean d'Haussonville

When the château was under construction, François I had little if any interest in the creation of gardens; the only known piece of greenery dating back to that epoch is a humble vegetable patch. What mattered most to the king was to channel the Cosson River, which crosses through the estate, rendering marshy the surroundings of the castle. He went so far as to envision diverting the nearby Loire so that Chambord would become an islet in the middle of the river. These projects did not materialize. It was much later, under the reign of Louis XIV, that garden landscaping around the building began in earnest. The sovereign placed an order with Jules Hardouin-Mansart, who got started in 1684. He began by filling the wetlands bordering the monument to render it less flood-prone, and fenced in the newly formed terrace with stone walls. But then, all of a sudden, work was indefinitely—and lengthily—suspended. Around 1730, at a time when Stanislas Leszczynski, the exiled king of Poland was sojourning in Chambord, the stagnant standing waters were propitious to mosquito proliferation and were causing malaria epidemics. During the summer, wishing to avoid potentially deadly fever, he took refuge in nearby dwellings in Ménars, Blois and Saint-Dyé, and warned the king's building inspector about this loathsome disamenity. In 1734, Louis XV demanded the pursuit of landscaping projects around the castle. The Cosson was dredged and widened to form a canal, bridges were built, and walls were erected on the river shore. A French-style garden was planted, covering close to fifteen acres. Starting in 1745, Maurice, count of Saxony, who after repeated sojourns wound up spending the last two years of his life in Chambord, enriched the garden. He planted boxwood and chestnut trees as well as bowers and plants in containers along the alleys. All told, there were 250 pineapple stalks,

121 orange trees, and two types of lemon trees. Shortly afterwards, a lawn was redesigned in the eastern section and two rows of flower beds were divided into squares with a well in the center of the composition.

The French Revolution meant neglected gardens; those in Chambord were no longer maintained. The alleys were overrun with weeds, the flowerbeds replaced by fruit trees or made to lie fallow and the desiccated castle moats turned into a vegetable patch. When the estate became the property of Henri, count of Chambord, and his inheritors, the garden had reverted to its simplest form: lawns with rudimentary flower beds, sanded alleys and rows of shrub clumps and thickets. In the early twentieth century, the garden was divided into long rectangular lawns, with a few trees; some alleys were adorned with yews, and a few rose trees subsisted in front of the castle. In 1970, these sparse growths were eradicated; only a few green spaces remained. Two years later, the moats were replenished. And then, in 2016, on the initiative of Jean d'Haussonville, estate director, the gardens were recreated and restored to what they had been, two centuries previous. The project was conducted by the architect Philippe Villeneuve, assisted by the landscaper Thierry Jourd'heuil and financed through the philanthropy of Stephen Schwarzman, the American billionaire. Managed by Pascal Thévard, the person in charge of the buildings and gardens of Chambord, the massive undertaking mobilized one hundred workers for eight months. All told, within and around eighteen thousand square meters (four and one-half acres) of turf they planted six hundred trees, eight hundred shrubs, two hundred rose trees and more than fifteen thousand plants delineating the borders, eleven thousand perennials and eighteen potted lemon trees. Today's gardens constitute an exact replica of those sketched out in the eighteenth-century plans, but they now benefit from an eight-mile-long, ultramodern, automatic watering system buried underground which draws the needed five thousand cubic meters (1.32 million gallons) of water a year from those of the Cosson River. Only a few plant species were replaced to adapt to a changing climate or for phytosanitary reasons, namely horse chestnut trees and boxwoods, which have in our regions been diseased for several years, and were replaced by ninety-two hundred thyme plants so as to reconstitute the flowerbed borders. On March 19, 2017, the French gardens were officially inaugurated by the president of the Republic François Hollande.

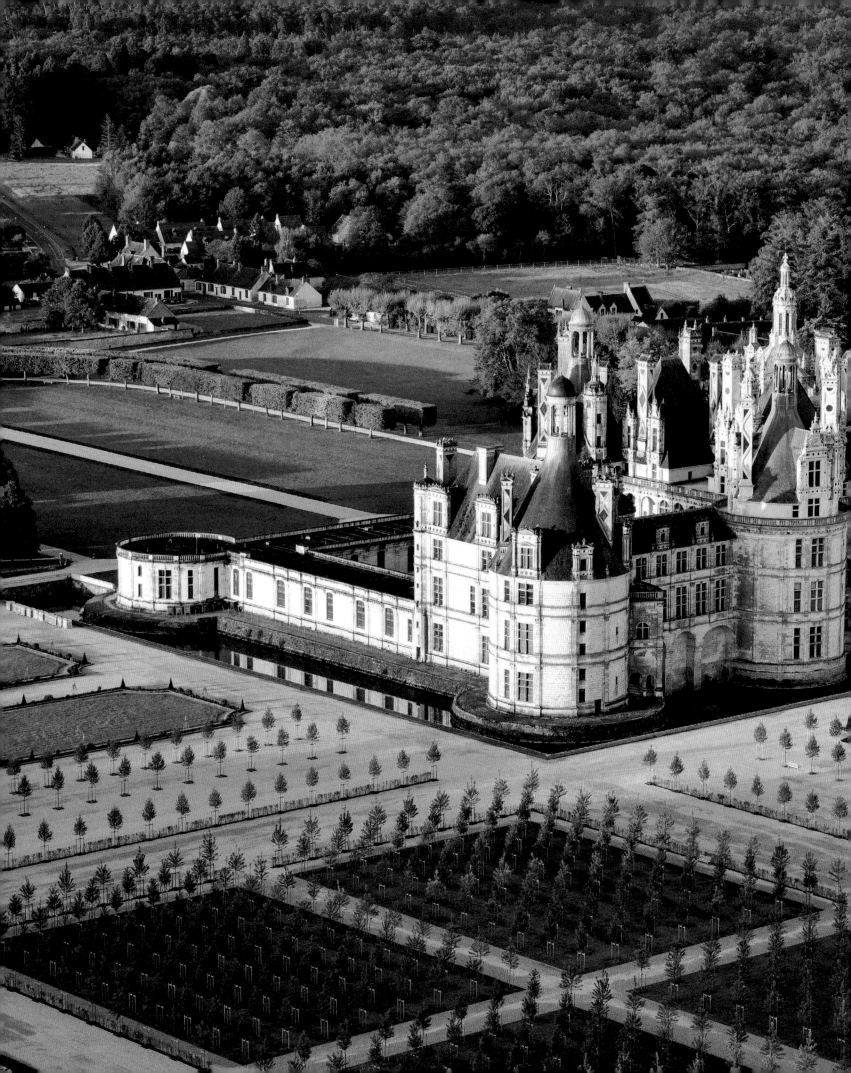

MORE HISTORY
IS HIDDEN
IN THE TREES

——

Since its creation by François I, the park has undergone substantial growth. With an area equal to Paris proper, its thirteen thousand acres and twenty-mile enclosure wall, completed in 1650 by Gaston, duke of Orleans, render it the largest closed and protected domain in Europe. In the Chambord estate, the château is by no means the only element steeped in history; the domain likewise perpetuates the memory of consequential human activity that has evolved over the centuries and persists in our times. Experts have counted out around 130 "modern" sites embedded under a mound, in a watercourse or a ditch, including hamlets, farms, lodges or *cul-de-loup* (the name given to the flimsy dwellings of loggers or coalmongers), medieval fortresses, a tilery and a dam. Many of these have disappeared, and their only remaining traces appear in the names of the cantons into which the park is split, or the buildings still standing. For example, *Les Charbonniers* is where charcoal used to be produced; until 1403 the *Parc aux Juments* (mare stable) contained the stud farms of the counts of Blois; *La Grande Faisanderie* is where pheasants were bred; *La Briquerie* is a one-time tilery; *Les Comte Thibault*, a medieval fortress; *La Motte de Vienne* was just a feudal clod, a modest stone and wood tower propped up on a mound and girdled by a circular pit. The *Les Bonshommes* pond was originally burrowed by friars, so-called good men (*hommes bons*). Some places bear the name of whoever resided there: *La Baquetière* was the abode of Baquet, *La Thibaudière*, the home of Thibaud. Nature is likewise remembered: *L'Ânerie* is where donkeys were bred, their braying was heard in *La Ricanière* (in French *récaner* is the ancestor of *ricaner*, to titter or giggle), and the *Taille aux Renards* was where foxes (*renards*) were hidden in the coppice (*taillis*). Elm trees (*ormes*) grew in the *Ormage*, hazels in *Le Coudreau*, and pines in *Le Pinay*; *La Pièce du Chêne* was a field where but one large oak tree (*chêne*) remained, while *Les Brosses* was a plot

——

The Maurepas chapel.

of land overrun by underbrush (*broussailles*). *Les Ventes Malheureuses* (sorrowful sales) recalled the abusive cutting down of trees to shore up the coffers of Maréchal Berthier's widow.

Archeologists have discovered traces of a mill and a fishery along the Cosson. The mill was designed to control a river that was constantly capricious, leaving its bed higgledy-piggledy and splitting itself up into several branches. But the march of time has not shattered everything in its wake: at the heart of the estate, in the middle of the forest, the Saint-Marc de Maurepas chapel may have been erected prior to the sixteenth century. Up until the eighteenth century, every April 25 it was the site of a pilgrimage, with worshippers streaming in from Saint-Dyé-sur-Loire.

There used to be about thirty agricultural holdings in the park; two of them remain active. To the west, there is the L'Ormetrou (it contained a bored elm tree) with its vines and its winery. In 1517, François I had eighty thousand vine plants transported from Burgundy to Romorantin, from which the grape variety acquired the name. Far from ordinary, it has mysteriously stood the test of time, surviving the phylloxera outbreak that devastated French vineyards in 1870. In 2015, where once existed a vineyard, the National Estate of Chambord planted close to forty acres of vines, including an ancient and historically significant variety, derived from previously ungrafted vines,

so as to produce long-keeping, natural and organic dry white wine. And to the west of the park, the Le Pinay farm, the last remaining traditional holding on the estate, is mainly devoted to the cultivation of cereals. Situated between the Le Périou pond and the Cosson River, the La Guillonnière farm (a certain Guillon lived there), of which the barn is festooned with several hundred trophies, hosts banquets for the public. Transformed into a watchtower, its one-time bread oven allows visitors to observe animals during the mating season. Other smallholdings have been converted into bed-and-breakfasts, technical facilities or estate staff lodgings, one example being the seventeenth-century guard pavilions at every entrance.

In 1970, President Georges Pompidou had a hunting pavilion built on the shores of the *La Thibaudière* pond; it is a wood structure with its niche in the forest. Just like the park and the château, the village has been transformed over the centuries. In or around 1556, Henri II urged dignitaries to have mansion houses built. The duke of Montmorency consequently ordered construction of a residence south of the village; it would bear his name until 1810, when it was renamed "Lina," the nickname of Caroline, Maréchal Berthier's daughter. It is still visible in the southern lawn of the château, where estate administration members are currently lodged. Practically next door stands the *Maison des Réfractaires* (holdouts' house), thusly

Below: Entrance to the cellar of the ancient château of Montfrault.

Facing page: Top left, inside the Maurepas chapel. Top right, the calvary of Rond-Prince-Louis. Bottom, the chapel of Maurepas.

Above: The *La Guillonnière* farm.

Facing page: Each road,
roundabout, prairie and pond
possesses its own plate.

Following double-page:
At the forefront, the *Neuf* pond;
in the center, the *Bonshommes* pond;
and, in the distance, the village
and the château.

The Pavillon de la Thibaudière,
east of the estate, pavilion
commissioned by President
Georges Pompidou.

named in memory of the village inhabitants who hid in the forest during World War II to escape induction in the STO (the mandatory work service). The building faces the stables of Maurice, count of Saxony, of which only ruins remain; every year, they stand in as backdrop for a horse show.

Since the opening of the château to the public in 1821 by the count of Chambord, the village has grown. The provisional stables set up in the late seventeenth century have evolved into the Place Saint-Louis, with its hotel and its merchants. Once annual attendance had reached and exceeded one million, in the early twenty-first century, the village had been modernized, with a new reception area and an extensively renovated hotel.

Throughout Chambord, the highways and by-ways are imbued with history, and even the most distracted visitor cannot possibly get lost! The park is checkered with roads, rings and roundabouts, all of which possess their cast iron plate. It was the count of Saxony who first undertook the patterning of the southern part of the forest, but only under the supervision of the count of Chambord, who gave instructions to the estate steward from his site of exile, was the gridwork finally completed. Moreover, the toponymy of a large number of thoroughfares is connected with a family and its history. For example, the *Route de l'Oubli* (Forgetfulness Road), in the heart of the forest, owes its name to Claude-Emmanuel Joseph Pierre, marquess of Pastoret, one-time tutor of the count of Chambord. After having refused, in accordance with the promises he

had made to the count, to pledge allegiance to Louis-Philippe, he wound up endorsing the latter's government, which is how the route came to be renamed. Another road, long and winding, serving several farms that no longer exist, departing from the château toward Orléans, was evocatively named the *Route de Jeanne-qui-sauve* (Joan the Savior's Road); it was finally replaced by a comparably long but straight-lined *Route de la Commission*, the commission being a fifty-member panel tasked with collecting subscriptions to buy the château from the princess of Wagram and offer it to Charles X for his grandson, the presumptive Henry V (count of Chambord). Once it opened, neighboring villagers were discontented; either the highway deprived them of a roadway, or they felt they had been robbed of their property; for whatever reason, as poachers or wood thieves might have done, they took to making dents in the wall. The royal administration contemplated putting up gallows to frighten the perpetrators.

Ardently desired by François I, the wall has constituted a continual cause for concern. In our times, it suffers not from malicious acts, but rather from the ravages of time and inclement weather; permanent attention must be paid, and costly repair work is often in order. The wall is not only an abiding remnant of historically noteworthy architecture, but also a protector of biodiversity in this thriving territory.

THE ART OF KEEPING
AN EXCEPTIONAL TERRITORY ALIVE AND WELL

"To conserve over the coming century, as it is, the forest of Chambord, at least as a testimony, were global warming to produce its feared deleterious effects."

Jean d'Haussonville

The Chambord forest park has been registered since 1981 as a UNESCO World Heritage site and was classified in 1997 as a historic monument. In 1959, having taken note of the degradation of the forest, which had benefited from no upkeep since 1913, the estate established a plan for continuous management of its massif. Today, maintenance of the forest, a vital part of the *Domaine*, is carried out by workers and seconded staff from the ONF (the national forests office) and ONCFS (the national agency for hunting and wildlife). The woods basically consist of sessile or native oak trees and Scots pines. As is the case throughout central France, the oak trees have been suffering and are endangered by climate change. The key priority of the estate is to preserve the forest for the decades yet to come. Sustainable forestry is conducive to reasoned and durable use and management. As of now, the estate harvests approximately fifteen thousand cubic meters (five hundred thirty thousand cubic feet) of wood a year. As regards natural habitats, the forest comprises an unusual diversity of landscapes: wetlands, heathlands and broom-covered fields, timber land, coppice with standards and prairies; all of them are constantly attended to, and together they ensure the survival of equally diversified floristic (650 identified plant species) and faunal species. A member of the Natura 2000 European network, of which the vocation is to promote the survival of endangered species and their habitats, Chambord is the only French territory in which, given its extraordinary size and its being enclosed, it has been possible for animals' natural behavior to be allowed to persist. Scientific studies on the interactions between hunting and biodiversity are regularly programmed. Young wild boars are entrapped so as to undergo medical examination and are given an eartag and an electronic chip. As regards the larger animals, the deer and older boars, it is during *panneautages* (a capture technique in which, during *battues*, they are pushed toward giant nets) that they are examined, marked,

Each year the estate processes 15,000 cubic meters (530,000 cubic feet) of wood.

and made to undergo blood collection. And some of them, before being released, are equipped with a GPS collar to analyze their comings and goings.

When World War II finally ended, French forests with the exception of Chambord were decimated. In 1947, the estate became a national hunting reserve and wildlife sanctuary. As such, it would help to repopulate French and other European forests. For several decades, delivering a hundred animals a year, it was to become the one site specialized in stag recovery and transplantation. Nowadays, given the return of big game in other European locations, the mission of the Chambord reserve is to protect the genetic strains of stags and boars. In accordance with Sologne tradition, the estate's seven large ponds are open for fishing, in the autumn and winter, once every two to five years. Due to the pulling of the plug, a few days before, the water level drops. Fishermen then enter the water equipped with large nets to circle and capture the fish, the overall objective being to regulate the water bodies' ecosystem. While predatory species are destroyed, others repopulate different ponds on the estate or are sold to a canning facility. Threatened with extinction, the black bee, a species endemic to Sologne, has been afforded refuge in the forest with the installation of several apiaries. Harvested by a nearby beekeeper, its honey is sold to the château. To revive the prairies surrounding the castle, and to recall the eighteenth century, when Maurice, count of Saxony initiated sheep breeding, a grazing herd of Sologne sheep has been resettled by a shepherd from a neighboring village.

Facing page: Pond fishing, a Sologne tradition indispensable to the regulation of water bodies' ecosystems. There are pike and pike perches aplenty.

Following pages: Renewal of the estate with the installation of sixty hives, a herd of Sologne sheep, and a vineyard.

Panneautage: Captured in large nets, the animals are examined, marked, counted and in some cases equipped with a GPS collar.

A CRY
FROM THE
WOODLANDS

———

From the château's terraces, a rumbling noise can be heard resonating through the immense forest starting to be adorned with the colors of autumn. Roaring, raucous, deep-seated and powerful lowing and mooing: the bellowing of the stag. From late September through mid-October, it is mating season for the king of the estate. Early in the morning and at twilight, the visitor tramping across the woods, into the clearings of La Croix Guillonnière or L'Ormage, through the prairies of La Pièce de Chêne or Princesse Zita, will discover an astounding spectacle. Openly if not brazenly, herds of deer have taken up quarters. Does and fawns graze on the grass displaying relative indifference, occasionally interrupted by a male wishing to mate. The stags howl at the top of their lungs to mark their territory, to express their sexual arousal, and to impress their rivals. Seemingly carefree, the young stags set out to conquer the does, the older ones jealously protecting their herds, perhaps twenty heads, and at the same time coveting the females. But, when a stag, despite warnings and visual or auditory

"In the morning mist, beneath feral branches
That the winds of autumn fill with lengthy murmurs,
The rivals, the two stags go at it under cover:
From the time of night when their roving frenzy
Drives them straight toward the odorous doe,

Antler to antler, toe to toe."

"The bellows have died down; the wind has stopped lifting the leaves. The does wait ashiver, all alone in the dead forest."

Maurice Genevoix, *La Dernière Harde (The Final Herd)*, 1938

attempts at intimidation, becomes too insistently pushy, the rivals have it out with one another. Face to face, they thrust themselves forward with all their might and voluntarily, violently, collide. Their antler ramifications clash, rattle and clatter with a sharp noise, as though snapping shut. The combatants show no pity; while the surrender of the weaker is the most frequent outcome, for some stags it is a fight to the death. It may even happen that the antlers grow entangled and that both animals die of exhaustion. This is an intense and possibly harrowing period for the stag, during which, at once protecting the herd, endeavoring to mate and engaging in potentially mortal combat, he may lose as many as thirty kilograms (66 pounds). His is a non-stop struggle to affirm and display domination; as victor, he will become master of the herd, with the right to fecundate one female after another.

Following double-page:

A stag combat can be exceedingly violent, at times representing a fight to the death.

THE STAG'S
KINGDOM

——

In Chambord, the château is not the only royal residence; the forest is another, and the stag is its king. In his exceptional natural territory, he reigns over a profuse and diversified fauna. Vast and totally enclosed, the estate offers the tranquility and nourishment necessary to the survival and thriving of a wide variety of species: insects, amphibians, reptiles, birds and mammals. There are approximately one thousand identified deer, essentially stags and a few roebucks. The elaph stag (red deer) is the largest wild mammal of Europe. His social life is built around herds. During adulthood, males and females live separately from December until August. Each year during the winter, a stag loses its antlers, but they immediately grow back. Contrary to received wisdom, the number of ramifications (*andouillers*) does not indicate age; the antlers reach their peak when the stag is eight to ten years old, and then decline in volume.

Approximately two thousand boars reside in the estate of Chambord. While the females, the sows, live in groups (companies), the males are solitary, and they are easily recognizable due to their fangs transformed into tusks. They are omnivorous, with a special liking for acorns, chestnuts and mushrooms. Much of the time, they root around in the earth with their snouts, thereby transforming it into ploughed land. It is especially at night that they find their food, often close to the roads that cross through the estate. Seemingly peaceable, in fact the boar is an edgy and quick-moving animal equipped with an excellent sense of smell and an acute sense of hearing. More unexpectedly, in the region there exist around two hundred Corsican bighorn sheep, and they are divided into several herds. They first arrived in the 1950s, during a breeding program in mountainous areas. Many other mammals cohabit in the forest of

Chambord: wildcats, foxes, squirrels, badgers, hares and coypus. In the vicinity of the wetlands, attentive eyes may espy newts with serrated crests or the salamanders that served as emblems for François I. Magnificent dragonflies hover over the Cosson and the fish-rich ponds. Gigantic carps silently gobble up the neighborhood insects. Early in the morning or at sunset, when carnivores start to hunt, it is not unusual to see perch or pike springing up from the water. Glancing upwards, the observer will appreciate the flight of herons and egrets, emblematic birds of a ponded Sologne, crossing their paths with raptors on the lookout for prey. And rare migratory birds return every year from Africa, the biggest of which, the Jean-le-Blanc short-toed snake eagle (circaetus), has a wingspan of 1.80 meters (5 feet, 11 inches). Three couples reside in the park, essentially subsisting on snakes, of which they could consume up to four hundred during their sojourns in France. As for the

Above: stags and boars are the two most numerous species populating the estate.

Left: a crow and a fox on the Cosson.

Facing page: Following their arrival in the 1950s, Corsican mouflons (sheep) are now part and parcel of the estate landscape.

osprey, it feeds exclusively on the fish it captures on water surfaces. It had previously all but disappeared from the French landscape; even today, there exist just twenty-five couples in metropolitan France, including eight on the Chambord estate. And then there are three couples of booted eagles, which provide a remarkable air show during their courtship. Hen harriers, hawks and many other bird species populate the Chambord sky. Mallard ducks fly in squadron-like formations and set down on ponds where a kingfisher, with his blue feathers folded up, plunges beak first. Enhanced by the chants of warblers, skylarks and other whistlers, the forest's tranquility is disrupted by the pounding of a grey-headed woodpecker on tree trunks or the calls of a pheasant or caws of a crow. At nightfall, the hoot of the tawny owl reverberates from the heart of the forest to the towers of the château. And while swans slide down and across the canal, other species inhabit the main building; the attic is home to two hundred greater mouse-eared bats. Each year when the warm weather starts, thousands of swallows take possession of the terrace ledges and set up their nests. Amidst the twenty-five hundred acres of the estate open to visitors, public watchtowers have been installed for observation of the animals. But Chambord is not a zoo, and it takes discipline and patience to fully enjoy the wildlife the estate has to offer.

Above: Left, the short-toed eagle is the only raptor nourishing itself with reptiles alone. Right, an osprey in its nest.

Facing page: A couple of egrets in the Le Périou pond.

FOR THE PLEASURE
OF TWO MILLION VISITORS

———

The wish to associate light and music had already germinated in the mind of Leonardo da Vinci when he organized his grand festivities. Logically enough, it was in Chambord that for the first time ever, a sound and light show was brought into being. In the evening of May 30, 1952, President Vincent Auriol attended the world premiere of *Les Très Riches Heures de Chambord*. A dance of a thousand lights highlighted the facade with music by Maurice Jarre in the background, and actors' voices told the story of the monument. Its remarkable success served as a model for celebrated sites throughout the world. The château has evolved with its times. Since 2015, a visitor can "time travel" with HistoPad. An individual digital tablet associating virtual reality with a global positioning system enables discovery of the different rooms the way they were during the Renaissance. That said, the edifice has no monopoly on recent renewal; the forest has also been rendered more hospitable. Since 2017, over fifteen miles of pathways for walkers, cyclists and horseback riders have been added to those already existing in the open section of the estate. As for those who wish to discover wildlife, a guide can shepherd them through the park in the driver's seat of an all-terrain vehicle. Whether fascinated by history or lovers of nature or both, the two million tourists visiting Chambord year in and year out can discover the estate by exploring the château on their own. But that is not the only way; you can also be accompanied by a guide and, when curious enough, accede to closed rooms and explore their hidden nooks and crannies. You can stroll through the French gardens, row down the Cosson River and fly across the estate in a hot air balloon. In the autumn, from the observatories you can follow the roar of stags in search of a mate; in the winter, you will be enchanted by the magical Christmas settings; in the spring, you may go antiquing in the most illustrious yard sale in the entire region or sit back and enjoy the horse show; in the summer, as a music lover, you will have plenty to choose from: a prestigious classical music festival, a concert given by the horn school of Chambord or

———

Facing page: The footpaths and bike lanes allow exploration of the open part of the estate.

Below: Jump demonstration above the château by the 1st Parachute Hussar Regiment.

———

Facing page and below:
Each year, the May 1 flea market brings together hundreds of stallholders.

Above and following double-page: Flying in a hot-air balloon to discover Chambord and its forest remains an unforgettable experience.

an evening where you can dance to the rhythm of electro music. Throughout the year, theme-based or monographic exhibitions, including those given by the estate's artists-in-residence, are organized in the château, which is one on the most dynamic heritage sites for contemporary art. What is more, you can picnic on the lawns or go out to eat at one of the establishments on Place Saint-Louis. The one-time estate farms converted into holiday accommodations will allow you to sojourn in the heart of nature at a stone's throw from the castle. And if you wish to awaken with Chambord at the edge of your bed, all you need do is fall asleep at the Relais de Chambord. Facing the monument, bringing together comfort and refinement, the hotel was renovated by the renowned architect Jean-Michel Wilmotte and opened its doors in 2018. And if, when exiting Chambord, you wish to take home part of its soul, you can choose objects manufactured in the estate workshops or coming from the natural resources of the forest, from its trees and deer antlers, the honey of its beehives or one of the many exceptional products originating, most importantly, in the hands of local artisans.

Below: All year long, the château hosts exhibitions and different forms of entertainment.

Facing page: Top, the château viewed from a room in the Le Relais de Chambord hotel. Bottom, a family picnic on the southern lawn of the château.

Back in the 1960s, the automobile manufacturer Simca christened one of its legendary vehicles as La Chambord; today, on the other hand, the estate is determined to safeguard its name and image. Indeed, more than seventy brands all over the world associate themselves in one way or another with Chambord, more often than not without authorization: Norwegian salmon, Australian water, chocolate, liqueurs and even coffins.

Wishing to put an end to this practice, preserve its intangible heritage and develop new financial resources, the estate has registered "Château de Chambord" as its trademark. Along with other sources of revenue, by 2020 these additional funds will allow the estate to self-finance, and it will be possible, thanks to patronage as well, to optimally ensure its maintenance, protection and restoration.

Facing page: Major cycling events, such as the Tour de France and the Tour de Loir-et-Cher, regularly cross through the estate.

Above: The *Inter-Entreprises de Blois* challenge on the canal. At times the estate becomes a playground for amateur sports meets.

CHAMBORD, A VILLAGE
WITH A SINGULAR STATUS

——

During the French Revolution, when the château was pillaged and the furniture sold off, the monument remained intact. Three years later, the Chambord township was founded, but the château remained abandoned. In 1809, Napoleon gave it as a gift to Maréchal Berthier, but his widow, who was unable to maintain what had become a derelict edifice, wished to be rid of it. In 1819, Louis XVIII finally agreed to having the château put up for sale. Unfortunately, a group of speculators, known at the time as the "Black Gang," bought parcels of land, dismantled different structures, and were planning to pawn off the material they had recovered. Wishing to spare the château from a tragic end, Adrien de Calonne, *fourrier* (steward) of the royal residence, proposed a nationwide fund-raising drive, so that the castle could be given as a birth gift to the son of Charles Ferdinand, duke of Berry, whose assassination in 1820 had shocked the public, when the infant was but seven months old. The campaign was successful,

and on March 5, 1821, Henri, duke of Bordeaux and grandson of King Charles X, became the proprietor of the entire estate. Forced into exile in early childhood, he would never inhabit the château. He nonetheless kept an eye on it from different locations throughout Europe. He commissioned restoration work and, in September 1839, decided to be called count of Chambord. As early as 1840, the château was registered on the initial list of historic monuments. When the duke died, in 1883, the estate was inherited by his nephews, princes from the house of Bourbon-Parma. Due to their Austrian citizenship, in 1915 the estate was placed in receivership. On April 13, 1930, after eleven million francs had been paid to the inheritors of the count of Chambord, the château and the entire domain became a *Domaine National*. As a result, everything in Chambord belongs to the French state: not only the château, but also the dwellings, the municipal buildings, the mayor's office, the shops, and even the cemetery, in which the plots belong

not to the families of the deceased, but rather to the state. The 120 inhabitants are all tenants. And yet, Chambord remains a township with its mayor, who retains policing powers over the communal area and has a seat on the château's governing board. The municipality holds elections and weddings, which are reserved for local citizens, and is even the scene for petty squabbles and bickering. The Saint-Louis church, which neighbors the town hall, was built at the bid and behest of Louis XIV. Two of its priests achieved renown. In 1562, during the European religious wars, one of them was slain at the alter by the Huguenots. Centuries later, on August 21, 1944, after the resistance fighters of the Forces Françaises de l'Intérieur (FFI) had ambushed a German patrol, killing two of their soldiers, the Germans set fire to the school, the Saint-Michel hotel and the Lina pavilion, and shot four hostages in retaliation. Abbot Joseph Gilg, a man of Alsatian origin and a German speaker, accompanied the château staff; together, they managed to persuade the occupant not to destroy the château and the works from the national museum collections that have been protected there since 1939 ; they also prevented the execution of forty villagers.

To put an end to the multiple guardianships to which the estate was accountable—no less than eight French ministries over the years—and to streamline management, in 2005 the French state granted it the legal status of a public industrial and commercial undertaking, thereby creating a single management unit. While confirming its validity, the French Council of State came to the conclusion that the existence of a unified *Domaine* in the hands of the state in no way interfered with free administration by the territorial authorities. From 2014, the village underwent a metamorphosis with the renovation of Place Saint-Louis and the modernization of its shops, along with the opening of an entrance hall and the updating of the Relais de Chambord hotel, just across the road from the château. And given its association with the history of the castle, the village's coat of arms has recovered its character as a blazon, showcasing the salamander.

Facing page: Top, the Saint-Louis church, commissioned by Louis XIV, neighbors the mayor's office. Bottom, the small Chambord cemetery.

Above: A Chambord wedding.

UNDER THE PROTECTION
OF THE PRESIDENT OF THE FRENCH REPUBLIC

———

"Chambord possesses a true republican history. It is a history of nature where attachment to nature and biodiversity is reconnected with the tradition of hunting."

Emmanuel Macron, president of the French Republic, December 17, 2017

Chambord is more than just a monument; over the years, it has become an emblematic center of the fifth French Republic. From 1965 to 2010, presidential hunting parties were organized for the benefit of major figures from the political, diplomatic and economic spheres. They often fostered informal encounters allowing the guests to talk things over in a convivial setting, blending tradition and prestige, all the while complying with protocol and perpetuating a hunting tradition inherited from the royal model. In 1970, a presidential hunting committee came into being: it organized meetings and submitted guest lists to the chief of state. Georges Pompidou and Valéry Giscard d'Estaing, both of them passionate shooters, were the most assiduous. While François Mitterrand was no hunter, he believed that hunting parties fulfilled a role, and

had them continue. Considering the latter as a monarchically tainted privilege, Jacques Chirac transformed them into state-regulated events and in 2010 his successor, Nicolas Sarkozy, put an end to the practice. Today, it is at the invitation of the Estate that legislators, senior officials, diplomats, entrepreneurs and philanthropists participate in "administrative" hunting parties. Chambord's attraction is not limited to illustrious marksmen; John Fitzgerald Kennedy visited the monument at the age of twenty; Juan Carlos, in 1975, Elizabeth II, in 1979; in 1987, it was the site of a meeting between German chancellor Helmut Kohl and François Mitterrand; the year after, it was the turn of Princess Diana and Prince Charles. And then, following a law enacted in 2005, the National Estate of Chambord was officially placed under the high protection of the president of the Republic. At Christmas 2017, President Emmanuel Macron spent a private weekend at the estate with his family.

Left: Major Étienne Guillaumat, Chambord hunting and forest director, renders honors beside a day's hunting bag.

Below: Left, on March 19, 2017 ex-president of the Republic François Hollande inaugurated the new French gardens, flanked by Jean d'Haussonville, general director of the estate (left) and Guillaume Garot (right), president at the time of the board of directors. Bottom and at the right, president of the Republic Emmanuel Macron and his wife Brigitte during a private sojourn in December 2017 at the Chambord estate.

Facing page: The estate hosts numerous ceremonial military parades.

ACKNOWLEDGMENTS

I would like to thank Jean d'Haussonville, general director of the National Estate of Chambord, for his hospitality and confidence, as well as the entire staff of the estate and château for having unwaveringly facilitated my work. I am particularly grateful to Cécilie de Saint Venant, communications director, and her team—Pauline, Elodie and Alexandre—for their availability and their smiles; Virginie Berdal for her valuable expertise; and Pascal Thévard, director of buildings and gardens, Frédéric Villerot, estate superintendent, Yannick Mercoyrol Director of Heritage and Cultural Programming and Jérôme Pellé, at the bookstore, for their precious assistance. The following staffers transmitted to me their passion for untamed nature in the heart of the estate: Etienne Guillaumat, hunting and forest director and forestry officials Pierre Charpentier, Blaise Decrouy, Christian Gambier, Freddy Cariello, Philippe Hubert, Jacques Lefebvre, Benjamin Genty, Thierry Touchet and Pascal Blondeau.

For their support and constant cooperation, I am likewise grateful to Stéphane Bern, Monique Chatenet whose book is an essential reference, Jérôme Mansire and his bees, the adjutant Thierry Jungas and the gendarmes of the Chambord mounted police, Mikaël Dubois and his *Compagnons "du Vent"* hot-air balloon, Laurent Charbonnier for his precious advice, Eric Bindet and his Salamander, and the entire *Éditions de La Martinière* team: Corinne Schmidt, Virginie Mahieux, Laurence Maillet and Marie-Amélie Clercant, for their unfailing patience. I owe special thanks to my faithful friends and accomplices Cyril Hofstein, Gilles Bassignac and Stéphane Jouannest, my partner in our youthful escapades in the forest of Chambord. Last but not least, special thoughts for A6, Mila and Loky, and for those who have accompanied me day in and day out: Sylvie Robert, Elodie Grégoire and my children Adrien and Margot.

Graphic design and art work: Laurence Maillet
Translation from French to English: Jeffrey Arsham
Proofreading: Alison Kim Flageul

Abrams books are available at special discounts when purchases
in quantity for premiums and promotions as well as fundraising
or educational use. Special editions can also be created to
specification. For details, contact specialsales@abramsbooks.com
or the address below.

Printed and bound in Portugal
10 9 8 7 6 5 4 3 2 1

ABRAMS
The Art of Books

195 Broadway
New York, NY 10007
Abramsbooks.com

ISBN: 978-1-4197-3782-4

Photoengraving: Point 11
Printed in September 2018